DISCARD

PRICKLY PORCUPINES

by Shannon Zemlicka

Pull Ahead Books

Lerner Publications Company • Minneapolis

This book is available in two editions:
Library binding by Lerner Publications Company, a division of Lerner Publishing Group
Soft cover by First Avenue Editions, an imprint of Lerner Publishing Group
241 First Avenue North
Minneapolis, MN 55401 U.S.A.

Website address: www.lernerbooks.com

Words in *italic* type are explained in a glossary on page 30.

Library of Congress Cataloging-in-Publication Data

Zemlicka, Shannon.
        Prickly porcupines / by Shannon Zemlicka.
            p. cm. — (Pull ahead books)
        Includes Index
        Summary: Simple text and photographs introduce the
    physical characteristics, behavior, and natural defenses of
    the porcupine.
        ISBN 0-8225-0685-8 (lib. bdg. : alk. paper)
        ISBN 0-8225-0966-0 (pbk. : alk. paper)
        1. North American porcupine—Juvenile literature.
    [1. North American porcupine. 2. Porcupines.] I. Title.
    II. Series.
    QL737.R652 Z46 2003
    599.35'974—dc21   2001006410

Manufactured in the United States of America
1 2 3 4 5 6 — JR — 08 07 06 05 04 03

This prickly animal looks like
a hairbrush.

What is it?

This animal is a porcupine.

Most porcupines live in forests.

Porcupines are prickly because
they have *quills*.

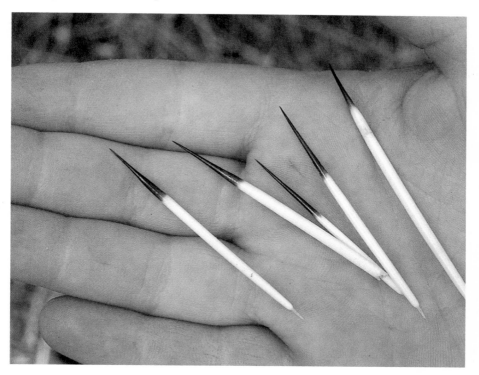

Quills are hard, sharp hairs.
They keep porcupines safe.

Look out, porcupine!
Here comes a coyote.

Coyotes are *predators.*

Predators hunt and eat
other animals.

What will the porcupine do
when it sees the coyote?

The porcupine turns around.

It curves its back to show its quills.
SWISH! It swings its tail.

Prickly quills can poke a predator.

OUCH! The coyote runs away.

The porcupine is safe.
It goes home to its *den.*

Porcupines sleep in their dens
for most of the day.

They leave their dens at night.

Porcupines find most of their food at night.

Sometimes they find food during the day, too.

Porcupines are not predators.

They eat plants, not animals.

Sharp
teeth help
porcupines
eat.

Claws help porcupines hold
their food.

What else do claws help
porcupines do?

Claws help porcupines climb trees.

Tree bark and leaves make good meals for porcupines.

Porcupines also eat plants that grow on the ground.

Porcupines eat and eat
all summer and fall.

They are getting ready
for winter.

There are no more leaves to eat when winter comes.

Then porcupines eat mostly bark and pine needles.

Spring brings
new plants
to eat.

Something else
happens in spring, too.

Baby porcupines are born in spring.

They are called *pups.*

Newborn pups *nurse.*

They drink milk from their mothers.

Mothers show their pups
how to eat plants.

This pup nibbles bark.

Mothers also show their pups how to climb trees.

Mother porcupines watch
over their pups.

They keep the pups safe.
How else do pups stay safe?

Pups are born with
soft quills.

The quills
become
hard and
sharp in just
a few hours.

This pup will show its quills if
a predator comes along.

Quills make growing up safe
for a prickly porcupine pup!

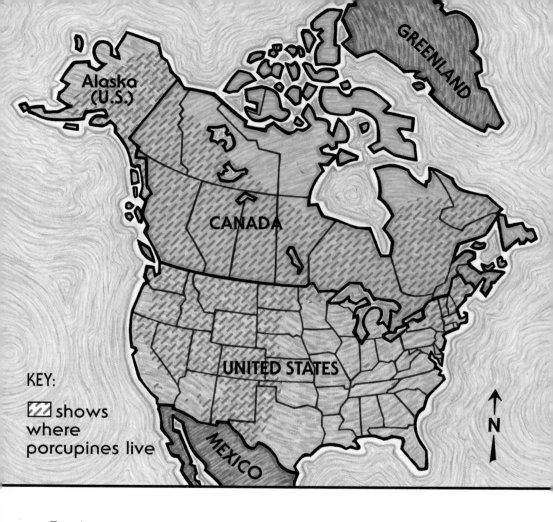

Find your state or province on this map.
Do porcupines live near you?

Parts of a Porcupine's Body

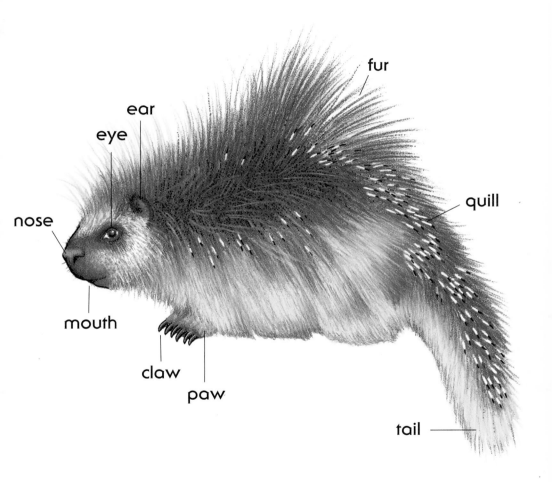

fur

ear

eye

nose

quill

mouth

claw

paw

tail

Glossary

den: a safe place where an animal sleeps

nurse: drink mother's milk

predators: animals that hunt and eat other animals

pups: baby porcupines. Baby porcupines are also called porcupettes.

quills: hard, sharp hairs that keep porcupines safe

Hunt and Find

About the Author

Shannon Zemlicka's first pet was a distant cousin of the porcupine. Ralph the guinea pig had no quills, but he did look a little like the porcupines pictured in this book. Shannon spends much of her time working with children's books as an editor and writer. She lives in Minnesota with her husband, two cats, and three dogs.

Photo Acknowledgments

The photographs in this book are reproduced with permission from: © Michele Burgess, pp. 3, 4, 7, 10, 11, 12, 13, 19, 21; © Alan & Sandy Carey, pp. 5, 16, 18, 22, 25, 26; © Anne Laird, pp. 6, 8, 9, 14, 15, 20, 31; © Leonard Lee Rue III, pp. 17, 24; © Len Rue, Jr., pp. 23, 27. Cover Photo: © Michele Burgess.